Milk Oh!

Bangers and Mash were playing on
the step of their house.
Along came the milkchimp.

He put two bottles of milk down on the step.

Then Bangers pushed Mash.

CRASH!

"Now look what you've done!" said Bangers. "All the milk has gone."

"No milk for tea. Mum and Dad will be angry with us," said Mash.

"I know what to do," said Bangers. "Come on!"

And off they went into the trees.

They went to see Sunflower the cow.
"We can take Sunflower home,"
said Bangers.
"Then we can have milk for tea."

It was not easy to get Sunflower up to the house.

It was not easy to get Sunflower
in the door.

Oh, Sunflower, what a mess!

"How do you milk a cow?" asked Mash.
"I don't know," said Bangers,
"but get a bucket."
So Mash got a bucket.

Bangers pushed Sunflower's tail
up and down but
no milk came out.

"That's wrong," said Mash.
"Try the other end."

But in came Mum and Dad.
"What's that cow doing here?" said Mum.
"It's the milk for our tea," said Bangers.

"And it's still in the cow!" said Mash.

What did you
eat yesterday?

Turn over and look
at the chart.

Don't write on it!

Are you getting enough calcium to make your bones grow strong?
You need to score 12 points on this chart.

	Points	Score
Breakfast cereal with milk	3	
A milk drink	5	
At least five cups of white tea or coffee	3	
A carton of yoghurt	5	
Hard cheese	6	
Custard or milk pudding	3	
Sardines or pilchards with bones	5	
Brown bread sandwiches	$\frac{1}{2}$	
White bread sandwiches	2	
Cottage cheese	1	
Baked beans	1	
Two servings of green vegetables	1	

Ask your teacher for a copy of this chart.

How to make Milkshakes.

Chocolate Milkshake

Stir 15 ml (3 tablespoons) of drinking chocolate
into a little hot water.
Cool.
Stir in 300 ml ($\frac{1}{2}$ pint) milk.
Pour into two glasses.
Put ice cream on top.
Serve with a chocolate flake bar.

Nutty Fruit Milkshake

Put 300 ml ($\frac{1}{2}$ pint) milk, one banana and
a carton of yoghurt (hazelnut) into a blender.
Switch on for one minute.
Pour into two glasses.
Put ice cream on top.

A page of jokes

What happens to a cow
if it sulks?
It gets in a moo-ed.

What do you call a cow
that sucks up dirt?
A moo-ver.

What happens to a cow
that is frightened?
It gets the milk shakes.

Why did the cow
go to the dentist?
To have its milk tooth out.

Where did the cow go
in the space rocket?
The Milky Way.

An old rhyme to learn

Hey diddle diddle!
The cat and the fiddle!
The cow jumped over the moon!
The little dog laughed
To see such sport

And the dish ran away with the spoon!

Mrs Snitchnose cast a spell
That made poor Sunflower quite unwell.
That nice cow she lost her moo.
When the farmer milked her the milk was blue.
Mrs Snitchnose laughed at her trick.
She laughed so much it made her sick.
While she was looking for a pill
Petal crept over the windowsill.
She found her spell book and her wand
And took and threw them in the pond.
Sunflower got better quite suddenly
And Petal and the chimps had milk for tea.

What does it mean? It's no use crying over spilt milk.
What does it mean? To wait till the cows come home.
Can you say? How now, brown cow, grazing in the green, green grass?
Can you say? You can milk a cow but you can't milk chocolate.
How many words can you find that rhyme with cow?

A Find-Out Page

Find out which foods are made from milk.

Find out which vitamins are found in butter.

Find out what these milk tops mean:

silver top

red and silver top

red top

blue and silver top

gold top

Find out how long UHT milk lasts.